FRUIT

First published in Great Britain in 2016 by
The Book Guild Ltd
9 Priory Business Park
Wistow Road, Kibworth
Leicestershire, LE8 0RX
Freephone: 0800 999 2982
www.bookguild.co.uk
Email: info@bookguild.co.uk
Twitter: @bookguild

Typesetting and cover design by Blacker Design, Sussex

Printed and bound in Great Britain by
CPI Group (UK) Ltd, Croydon, CR0 4YY

ISBN 978 1 910878 71 2

British Library Cataloguing in Publication Data.
A catalogue record for this book is available from the British Library.

FRUIT

Grow, cook and preserve your own

Rosemary Sassoon

The Book Guild

contents

FRUIT

Grow, cook and preserve your own

This is not going to be a traditional book of gardening instructions or even recipes, more a book of ideas to start you thinking. My garden is my real larder and inspiration. It provides fruit and vegetables most of the year, and after many years of practise, really does not take up too much time and energy. So my freezer and larder are full of produce and what I don't grow myself is often supplemented by hedgerow fruit.

Some of these ideas apply equally to anyone with an allotment, or even someone who likes to shop at their local farmer's market, visit pick-your-own farms in season, or spot bargains of seasonal fruit and vegetables elsewhere. Anyhow, some things cry out to be grown, and are easy and relatively trouble free to maintain. Some things need to be eaten almost as soon as they are harvested so are tasteless from shops, while others are so cheap and easy to buy, or perhaps do not prosper in your soil. Then it is simpler – and no disgrace – to buy them.

We cannot grow everything we eat, our climate amongst other things is against us. I could not do without citrus fruit or bananas, mushrooms, even main crop potatoes (lack of space), so we cannot claim to be totally self-sufficient, but we can do our best.

To give you an idea of what can be grown in a smallish garden or allotment without too much trouble I will deal with the fruits one by one, as they come into season.

If you can't grow all of these yourself they might be available at your local pick-your own farm or farmers market. The point is to enjoy as many fruits as possible in season and to conserve or freeze any gluts that arise, or any bargains you spot along the way.

RHUBARB

There are a surprising number of different types of rhubarb available, from very large to quite small varieties with slightly different flavours. Our plants came with us when, many years ago, we moved south from Yorkshire, the centre of rhubarb growing in England, where it is forced and mass produced in huge sheds. Rhubarb is so easy and satisfying to grow. Just plant a root or two and it goes on forever.

Early rhubarb comes in late March in good springs, otherwise early April. You can force the plants by placing a large pot over one or two of your sprouting roots to hurry them up and produce those delicate pale pink stalks. It may weaken the roots a bit, but it is worth it and you can always leave other roots to develop in their own time.

Those first few pink stalks are so delicious they need nothing more than cooking gently with a little sugar. With older rhubarb, which tends to get a bit sourer and tougher, you will probably need more sugar and you can enhance it with different flavours. Ginger is one, but there are other flavours. Try adding a small tin of passion fruit pulp or if you can't find that an orange or a couple of tangerines.

If you get a second flourish of rhubarb and it coincides with your red currants, the two flavours go very well together stewed or in pies or crumbles. If you want a change why not try a cobbler which would work well with rhubarb's strong flavour. Just make your usual pastry mix into a moister mixture and spoon, rather like scones, onto the top of your fruit before baking. You will find that the juice oozes through the channels in the topping making an easy and delicious pudding, specially when served with clotted cream.

A pastry base with the fruit then topped with meringue works well, also my version of apple charlotte (see page 28), where the fruit is lightly fried in butter and sugar, with cubes of bread cooked in the delicious syrup.

You can always sieve older rhubarb and make a fool with yogurt or cream, to be eaten fresh or frozen for another day, using plenty of sugar – or why not honey or maple syrup for a change. Rhubarb, orange and ginger jam is good too. If you have even more, you could make a relish or chutney. A recipe that I found on the back of a pack of sugar suggested using rhubarb and dates in (plus the usual onions, spices like ginger, or cinnamon) with vinegar and golden syrup in a chutney. Any excess after all this can be cooked and frozen to enjoy later on in the year, on its own or combined with other fruit such as apples or pears. Please do not be too inventive with rhubarb however – remember that their leaves are poisonous!

GOOSEBERRIES

For some reason gooseberries are difficult to find in shops so this is all the more reason to plant a bush or two in some corner of your garden. All they will need is occasional pruning and they could even be trained to make a nice prickly hedge to keep out intruders. There are many varieties, some green and some red, some better for cooking and others for ripening and eating raw.

Gooseberries give virtually two crops. I like gooseberries best when they are very young, just gently stewed with a little sugar and a few elder flowers. These are conveniently out in every hedgerow at the same time and their taste combines perfectly to provide an almost muscatel flavour. The longer you wait to cook the fruit, perhaps feeling that you should leave the gooseberries to get larger, the sourer they become when cooked, and the more sweetening they need. Many people only think of ripe gooseberries that once again become sweet and juicy to eat raw. They are delicious but not very good for cooking at that stage. In my garden the squirrels usually get them before they are sweet enough to enjoy raw, so I pick most of them when young, pack in bags before they soften and begin to ripen, and put in the freezer for use later on. Really professional gardeners have fruit cages and then they have more choice as to when they pick.

Gooseberries are one of my best standbys. They are always ready for unexpected visitors. Pour some out of a freezer bag, add a cube of elderflower juice if you have managed to keep some, and boil with sugar. Just liquidise or sieve – I use a mouli as it removes the pips, and add cream or yogurt to taste. The resulting fool, or soft frozen ice cream are always favourites. Do not be confined by my ideas alone. Try whatever mixture of fruits you happen to have around. Not long ago I decided to make a quick fool. Before reaching for the elderberry syrup, see page 8, I noticed some rather substandard strawberries, the remainder of a picking during a dry spell. I stewed the gooseberries as usual, then strained off most of the juice. The strawberries were stewed in that and then strained and generously sweetened. This scarlet syrup went into the sieved gooseberries, cream was added and an unusual pink dessert resulted. Some quartered strawberries, marinated in a little more of the syrup, made it look a bit more elegant.

Young gooseberries make a delicious jam. Cook and sieve older fruit to make jelly. Flavoured with elderflower, either jam or jelly are even more delicious enhanced by its slight muscatel flavour. They are good to accompany meat, even fish as well as to spread on toast or scones. Stewed gooseberries are a traditional accompaniment to mackerel. They counter the richness of the fish. Gooseberry juice is a useful vehicle for other flavours such as mint see page 22, for instance.

Gooseberries are the most versatile of fruits. You can put them in pies, top them with crumble, or combine with other stewed fruit, apples in particular or add them to fruit salads and summer pudding mix. With their robust flavour they are good in flans or open tarts. You can reduce some juice to set, or use a little gelatin to glaze them, or try topping them with meringue. With some golden syrup they would make a good upside-down baked sponge pudding.

STRAWBERRIES

Strawberries are everyone's favourite fruit – harbingers of summer and lazy days in the sun. There is nothing like the flavour of your own fruit and the thrill of picking a bowl full when all goes well. However, there are pros and cons about growing them. They are somewhat of a high maintenance crop compared with many other fruits. They are so easily available that I sometimes wonder if it is worth the trouble of growing them. To be honest, they are quite a lot of work. The plants need renewing every two or three years (from their own maiden runners, those off the one year old plants) and they are often victims of unseasonable weather. The fattest get mildew if there is too much rain and should be bedded in fresh straw to help avoid just that, and occasionally they dry up in very hot years. Slugs, birds and squirrels love them and it is a constant battle, even when you think you have netted them sufficiently.

One great advantage of strawberries, unlike most fruit, is that you are ensured of a crop after only a year. So, in the early years of my marriage when we moved house frequently, the strawberry bed was the first thing to be planted. Like everything else, they do better with a dressing of compost and mine get their share of ash as well from the nearby bonfire, to supply free potash.

I am not a perfectionist gardener. There is seldom enough time or energy these days to do what I ought, like spreading straw underneath my berries, as I used to do when younger, (even that does not absolutely ensure perfect fruit whatever the experts say). As a result by no means all of my fruit is perfect and I divide my pickings accordingly. Perfect fruit needs no help but cream and sugar but they do not keep their glossy perfection for much more than twenty four hours. If you want to keep them longer it is a good idea to macerate them. This means slicing them when fresh and covering them with sugar. Mix well together and soon the juices will begin to flow and this way your fruit will keep well for several days in the fridge

There are plenty of uses for less than perfect strawberries. If you feel energetic try pavlovas (meringues) filled with strawberries. They improve by being marinated in sugar and something alcoholic. The next best fruit I often mash or liquidise, add plenty of sugar and yogurt plus a little cream. This concoction is delicious and quite hard not to eat straight away, but I try to resist and save enough to put in ice cream containers to freeze. It makes a welcome dessert when guests arrive later on in the year. It can be eaten frozen like ice cream or softer more like a fool. For that matter, why always add cream or yogurt when the liquidised fruit alone could be frozen and treated like a kind of granita. That lovely exotic name just means something juicy, frozen and then thawed to whatever state you like.

Less than perfect fruit can also be used in the filling for a strawberry shortcake. Just make two sponge cakes, then slice the fruit, sweeten with sugar and tip into some whipped cream, Sandwich this mixture between the two cakes, having cut a circle in the top of the cake to reveal the contents. Add some perfect fruit to the top. You can spend as much time as you want decorating it, piping cream and arranging the fruit – it will disappear just as quickly whatever you do! Your strawberries do well in traditional trifles either with your own jam or fresh.

Use strawberries in milk shakes or smoothies and fruit salads. Summer salads can include fruit as well as the usual ingredients, so try adding a few strawberries to tomato, lettuce, cucumber and whatever else you have around. This is another use of less than perfect fruit. I have never tried to freeze whole, perfect strawberries but I am told that if you spread them carefully on a tray, pointed end upwards, then they freeze successfully, Left to myself I would say that whole strawberries do not freeze particularly well. So, if I have too many to use straight away, (which is not often), and not much space left in the freezer, I would prefer to liquidise them and freeze, to defrost and add sugar and cream and use in some way, usually as my usual sort of ice cream/frozen dessert, later on.

I have just tried another variation of freezing, inspired with what happened with my gooseberry/strawberry dessert (see page 5). I have gone on to quarter some good strawberries cover them with similar strawberry/gooseberry syrup and freeze them in small containers for use in fruit salads or elsewhere in the winter. I found that they retain the taste of fresh strawberries and will try them again next year. If you start experimenting with whatever you have you will soon develop your own recipes.

If you feel like a dramatic summer drink try something like this: Cut up some strawberries quite small and marinate them with sugar and a bit of lemon juice or something stronger if you like. Pop some into individual glasses or a glass jug and top up either with white wine, for adults or perhaps white grape juice and fizzy water or even apple juice if you cannot find anything else. This would be a great hit at a children's party. To make it better still some borage flower and mint could be sprinkled on top. Borage seeds itself year after year, and apart from being an attractive and decorative flower, it is wonderful for attracting bees to your garden.

The flavour of oranges go well with strawberries, so you could try adding orange juice to any of your ideas, whether a drink, poured over sliced fruit, added to your liquidised mix to freeze or use as a sauce on ice cream.

Then there is the matter of jam. There are many methods all trying to get this delicious fruit, which lacks pectin, to jell. The simplest method is to melt a little sugar in the juice of a lemon in the bottom of the pan and slowly add the fruit and sugar (without water) in the usual proportion: 1 pound of sugar to one pound of fruit. Boil until setting point and cheat by adding pectin if you wish.

This way used to be so easy because I used to grow special small, more pectin-rich jam strawberries called little scarlets. They are not generally available as those who bred them make their own very successful commercial brand of conserve. Sometime, way back, they let one of my aunts have some plants – in exchange for something else, I suspect. They were a menace to control and took over the place, and gradually I found them too much hard work, and only keep a few under the fruit trees for sentimental reasons (and for the benefit of the birds).

There is another quite different way that I have tried. It consists of putting your fruit and sugar together in a large bowl and putting it in a warm oven for ten minutes. Then you take this out and mix together for another ten minutes before returning it to the oven. This procedure should be repeated at least four times. It is time consuming but results in a wonderful conserve of whole strawberries in syrup and should set too, with luck.

One year a disaster prompted yet another method. A huge crop of berries was just on the verge of ripening when there was a fortnight of blazing sun with temperatures well into the eighties every day. My strawberries just dried up before my eyes but I could not bear to waste these poor dessicated things. Luckily there were a lot of red and white currants that year so I used them to make a jelly. The dried strawberries were immersed in this and rehydrated somewhat when boiled. Then the whole mixture was put in a sieve to drain, and measured for sugar. The resulting jelly was perfect – tasting of strawberries but rather sharper than the usual jam, and it set perfectly. This made me think that I might try this again some year. I did something similar in another hot dry season which resulted in a lot of dried up strawberries, but this time I had not been quick enough with my nets and the birds had eaten all my currants. I tried using gooseberry jelly instead and it was just as successful. Apple would be just as effective as they have plenty of pectin in them – but they are not usually in season at the right time.

Another hot year, as we live in Kent surrounded by fruit farms, my daughters hired themselves out as strawberry pickers. Some of the fruit was just too overheated to sell. Still perfectly good to eat, it was set aside in buckets to throw away. We rescued it, took it home and boiled it up. The resulting juice was a great success and did not last long enough to try adding lemon or other juices to the mixture. I am sure there would be plenty of opportunities for experimenting should such an occasion ever arise again.

You could also try freezer jam, which means mashing your fruit with approximately the same weight of sugar and blending well together. This delicious uncooked mix needs to be stored in small containers in the freezer because it only keeps good for a few days when defrosted.

People ask me what kind of strawberries I now grow, because there are so many different commercial varieties.. Their story is this: we were in South Wales, many years ago, and found a small, isolated bed and breakfast place high in the hills. As we arrived our host was tidying up his strawberry bed and had a healthy pile of runners that he was about to put on the compost heap. It seemed a shame, and the runners were subsequently neatly parcelled up for us. When I enquired what sort they were it transpired that the couple were retired strawberry farmers from Hampshire and they had bred and developed them specially for themselves. I have grown them ever since. I look on a garden as a kind of living autograph book. Plants and cuttings are exchanged and grow on to remind you of the friends and family who gave them to you.

CHERRIES

Cherry trees have such beautiful blossom, we were lucky to have several old ones which have now gone – but they were big old fashioned ones and the birds got most of the fruit. Their replacements are all on dwarf stock which can be more easily protected from ravenous predators. If you have any reason to prune your cherry trees be sure to do it in the late spring or summer. Cherries, like all stone fruit, plums, peaches etc. should never be pruned when their sap is down. That means in the late autumn or winter.

There is little point in writing much about dessert cherries – they are so delicious raw that few people want to do more than just eat them straight away or perhaps spare a few to grace a special fruit salad. A friend made us a particularly delicious summer pudding. Not growing her own cherries she added bought dark red Spanish ones to the usual mix of raspberries and black currants which made me think that it might be worth cheating a bit sometimes. When I think a bit more about it, I do sacrifice a few cherries to pop into my frozen strawberry desserts where they make a welcome surprise later on, and if any were still about they would go well in the loganberry mould or a similar pudding, see page 20.

Morello cherries, ripening later, are another matter. As far as growing them, they are one of the few fruits that prosper when grown against a north-facing wall. As far as flavour is concerned it is unsurpassable. When fully ripe and almost black they can be eaten raw but they are usually reserved for cooking in one way or another. Just stewed, the are very special with their slight maraschino taste. The few containers of frozen morello cherries (there are never enough) are my absolute favourites, and are saved to cheer up the dark days of winter. Morello jam is perhaps the next best use, but I always save some to add to mixed cooked fruit, and to summer puddings if it is a good year and there are plenty. They add their special flavour to raspberries, blackcurrants and gooseberries or whatever is around. I freeze this concoction to keep a taste of summer for the long winter days. And what about crystallizing them?

If you have enough patience to remove their pips then morellos would make good shallow pies, or upside down puddings where their strong flavour would not take so much of your precious fruit. A sweetened thick juice (with or without cherry brandy) is delicious to pour over ice cream, or a special jelly with whole fruit or perhaps a few sliced peaches in it, would be delicious. I have seen various recipes which use cherry sauce with meat but have never tried this. Anyhow, if I only had space for one cherry tree it would be a morello because I have never found them on sale anywhere. (Living in Kent there are still cherry orchards so there are plenty of dessert cherries for sale – at a price).

Be warned again – it is very difficult to protect your cherries, whatever sort, from the birds who delight in destroying your precious crop before it is fully ripe, but do not let that put you off trying.

RASPBERRIES

This fruit really needs a chapter on its own. Easy to grow, versatile in their usage, raspberries can have a season lasting from late June to the coming of frost if you plant a few different varieties. Raspberries have a short shelf life – this means that they do not last long once they are picked. This is one of the main reasons, I suppose, that they are relatively expensive in shops. When I see the price of small punnets displayed in shops at the height of the season, I think of how easy raspberries are to grow. Although the birds take their share of the early ones if you do not net them, they leave the later ones alone. In my garden it is the later crop that yields the most and allows me to freeze or be more inventive with them.

The early varieties need to have the canes that have just fruited cut, to allow the new ones to develop. The autumn ones need to be cut right down to the ground in February and then left to themselves to get on with growing. Like everything else, they appreciate a bit of compost spread in the spring, or wood ash from the bonfire – but by no means do mine get that every year. Most canes need some support. One or two strands of wire will keep them in order. This applies particularly to the autumn varieties which can grow very tall.

If I could only grow one fruit it would be raspberries. Freshly picked they are perfect alone with cream, ice cream or yogurt, on any cereal or muesli for the ideal breakfast and so many other ways. They are an essential ingredient of summer puddings so let's start there: For a summer pudding you need enough sliced bread (preferably a little stale) with crusts removed, to line your dish. It is surprising how much stewed fruit you need, so be prepared, and stew gently and sweeten a mixture of whatever you have available – raspberries of course, blackberries, and a few plums, gooseberries, blueberries, loganberries, or whatever is about depending on the season, even a few apples – but preferably mostly red fruit.

Make sure there is plenty of juice. I moisten the bread carefully in the juice before replacing it and filling with fruit and juice – otherwise some pieces may not get soaked right through and come out pale pinkish. Make sure you keep enough juice for the top bread which is most in need of being immersed, before completing the pudding. Pour on any remaining juice, place a plate on top of it all and weigh it down with something heavy.

It is ready to eat when cold or, as I often do, freeze, for future use, having used an ice cream container instead of a dish. You can also make dainty individual summer puddings. They would use proportionately more bread and make the fruit go further, but I have never had the patience to try. You could also make individual cold souffles or mousses using raspberry (or strawberry for that matter) puree instead of the more usual lemon.

For winter fruit salads I freeze excess perfect soft fruit, whole and uncooked, in plastic bags in the freezer – raspberries, currants particularly black ones, gooseberries, blackberries but not strawberries. When needed all I do is to get out the desired amount of raspberries and let them begin to defrost. Then I take a generous amount of blackcurrants (because their strong flavour seems to give something special to the mix) and anything else uncooked that is still in the freezer like gooseberries or blackberries, even plums. Those will go into a saucepan with some sugar and when cooked are ready to pour over the raspberries and complete their defrosting. It all only takes a few minutes and then you can add any spare bananas or perhaps pears that need eating up, as you wish.

Perhaps I should explain how I sort out the fruit if I have a big picking — as I do more often with autumn fruiting canes. The very best are frozen, then the next best are eaten fresh which leaves the slightly damaged or not so good fruit to be juiced for jelly (which we prefer to pippy jam) or sieved and sweetened and frozen as juice. When the juice is to be kept

for drinking it is always prepared with as little water as possible – just a spoonful or so, so it takes up as little space as possible when bottled and kept in the freezer. My juices are often a mixture of fruits perhaps with blackcurrants with the midsummer raspberry crop or grapes with the autumn ones. Of course this can also be used as a granita or frozen or a part-frozen dessert.

Now for jellies and jams: In my children's summer holidays we spent several periods of raspberries picking. That way we learned more of the ins and outs of the trade and have avoided bought raspberry jam ever since. Much of the crop was sent to producers who added something to them that bleached them before freezing. They then had to have something else added to give them back their colour before ready for jam. I do not know if that is still allowed but it has put us off bought raspberry jam forever.

When it comes to preserves many people, including me, prefer to exclude raspberry pips and make jelly. Jam is simple though, just add the usual proportion of fruit to sugar and boil, or, alternatively try freezer jam which is just fruit and sugar, uncooked, and mixed together until the sugar dissolves. Frozen in small pots (yogurt pots for instance) this method preserves the taste of fresh raspberries. There is a definite difference between cooked and uncooked fruit. It is a matter of which you prefer but a small pot of freezer jam makes a special gift to a child in bed with flu or perhaps an adult with some more serious illness, but you have to remember that it does not stay good for long once it is defrosted.

When it comes to jellies there are plenty of opportunities

to experiment and, if necessary, to make your fruit go further. Start with simple raspberry jelly which is just as good as strawberry jam (with cream) on scones. Adding red currants makes a slightly sharper jelly, and raspberry and crabapple jelly is good too. What you try depends on what is around at the time – your raspberries are infinitely obliging and versatile.

More unusual is raspberry and rosemary jelly which I first found at a herb farm in Australia. All you do is to add a small bunch of fresh rosemary to your hot juice and leave for a few minutes. Then sieve, measure and add the sugar in the usual proportions of a pound to a pint, and a small amount of vinegar. I suppose this is meant for eating with meat and especially game, but I like it just as much on toast or bread, and so do many of my visitors – try it.

And then there is juice – either raspberry alone or combined with black, red or white currants or whatever is around, even grapes as I found one year when our vine did unexpectedly well. I try to make any juice as condensed as possible to save space. Bottled in small plastic water bottles they are stacked in the freezer and drunk either hot or cold, with plain or fizzy water. It only takes a minute to pour some boiling water in a bowl and defrost a bottle for an unexpected guest, and you will never feel the same about bought fruit juice again.

Raspberry juice has other uses too. For children, use it to make home-made iced lollies in those plastic shapes that are easily available. Why not make real jellies by adding gelatin – you can get vegetarian gelatin if necessary – to raspberry juice. Then you or your children, can pop a few whole fruit, or perhaps a peach to add to the appeal.

What is that fashionable word 'coulis' other than reduced or thickened juice. You can make your dessert or ice cream look expensive by dribbling it in patterns – or delicious by generously pouring over this concoction enriched, if you like, with a little brandy or fruit liqueur. You can make your own ice cream quite simply. Mix your raspberry juice or puree with cream, or preferably half cream half yogurt, and freeze making sure to get it softened enough before serving. To make it smoother for those of us who have not got an ice cream maker, you can defrost your mixture and put it in the liquidiser before re-freezing it. A healthier alternative would be a raspberry sherbet or granita, just right for the occasional hot summer day, served with a sprig of mint and a dish of freshly picked fruit or a fruit salad.

Raspberry vinegar takes a lot of fruit, said the friend who often gave me some as a present. This was a fair exchange for the canes that originally came from one of my aunts' garden. There are always extra canes after a few years as many varieties spread rapidly and would take over half a garden if left on their own. There is something special about sharing plants out of your garden – to my chagrin, when I give people plants they usually manage to get them to prosper better than I can do in my garden. I suppose that you can buy raspberry vinegar but I doubt if it would have as intense and delicious flavour as your own home made. A little poured on a summer salad makes all the difference – my summer salads often have summer fruits added to the usual tomato, cucumber and lettuce ingredients.

LOGANBERRIES

These are a cross between raspberries and cultivated blackberries. They grow from the root on long stems that need to be trained along a wire and cut off when they have fruited (otherwise they would end up like an unruly bramble patch). When really ripe and dark purply black they are delicious to eat raw, but their real value is revealed when cooked. They have such a strong flavour that you do not need many berries to add to any mix for eating cooked or in a summer pudding. A favourite recipe, inherited from another aunt made particular use of loganberries. Stewed and pureed the fruit is thickened with a little arrowroot. (I suppose cornflour would do or even gelatin, but it would not be quite the same). When poured into a shallow dish, she sliced a peach into the mixture before letting it set. It is a lovely combination of flavours and has become a family favourite. You could experiment with other sliced or whole fruit like a ripe pear, or those delicious morello cherries which are ripe at the same time, but we just keep to the original idea out of sentiment, I suppose.

If you only have a few loganberries then use as them as a sauce (fortified by a liqueur if you like) to pour over ice cream. If you have lots of them spare some to make jam or jelly.

CURRANTS

There are red, white and black currants, each with their special flavour and uses. They all grow on bushes and grow easily, only needing protection from voracious birds whose favourite food they seem to be. The main difference between them is that red and white currants need exactly the opposite kind of pruning to black currants. The first two fruit on old wood so need to have the new shoots shortened – sort of pollarded. You never shorten the stems of black currants as they fruit mainly on new wood, but you cut out single branches when they get too old and long, and the bushes too crowded.

Some people delight in red currants and even more the sweeter white currants in fruit compotes and summer puddings. Others find them rather sour and pippy. No one, however, would deny their decorative value on top of a special dessert or cake.

Everyone knows about red currant jelly to be eaten with meat and game or your Christmas turkey if you have forgotten the cranberry sauce, but if you have never tried home-made red currant jelly just on toast, you have missed a treat. It is simple to make and sets easily. You would add a bit of vinegar if you intend to use it with meat, or keep just to sugar for everyday use.

Cumberland sauce, the perfect accompaniment to game of any kind uses red currant jelly as an essential ingredient. An old friend always gave pots of Cumberland sauce as a most acceptable Christmas present. Traditional recipes suggest using about 1 lb redcurrant jelly, 2 juiced oranges and lemons plus the rind of one of each, to 2 glasses of port or red wine but I would think that you could personalise your sauce to suit yourself.

White currants make a delicious sweet jelly and can be used in other ways as well. I use it as a as a base for mint jelly. Apple jelly is more usual for this but when mint is at its best the apples are not ready. Thinking of other uses (see strawberry and currant, or any other varieties of jelly on pages 10 or 18) morello cherries would also be delicious and decorative immersed in white currant jelly, so would loganberries. I must try it when I next beat the birds to a good crop.

Black currants may share a name but are a very different fruit. People either love or hate their strong, distinctive flavour. I use my frozen hoard in winter in fruit salads. The simplest way, when I am in a hurry, is to take out a bag of raspberries and put them in a basin to start defrosting. Then some black currants (plus gooseberries and loganberries if wanted) are put on to cook with enough water and sugar to ensure a good syrup for the fruit salad. When it is poured on to the raspberries it will complete defrosting them and a luxurious dessert is ready for the unexpected guest in a very short time. It goes without saying that a bottle of black currant juice is always welcome, cold in summer and hot in winter. When I get bored with plain stewed windfall apples, a few spoons of blackcurrant juice – or a handful of frozen fruit – liven it up.

What may not be realised, when you may be put off by the cost of black currants in shops, is the effect of their very robust flavour. You need very little to flavour a milkshake, yogurt or ice cream mix. When I make my usual frozen dessert with black currants, I cook them first but do not sieve them. A friend gave me a very economical recipe for black currant jam. It consisted of using three pints of water to one pound of fruit to four pounds of sugar instead of the usual proportion of perhaps one pound of fruit to one of sugar. It works well that way, and sets too. Another friend of mine has a completely different use for black currants. She makes delicious muffins for her guest's breakfasts. They are probably a variation of American blueberry muffins. Maybe, like me, her blueberry bushes refuse to flourish.

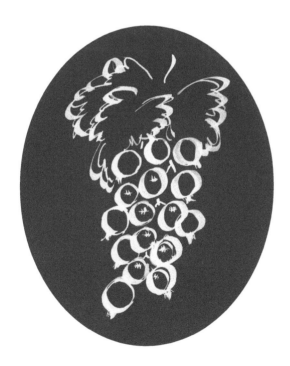

PLUMS

I have several plum trees, planted over the years. The Victoria is everyone's favourite – the best for eating raw or, we think, for cooking. Then we have an old tree of large dark blue fruit, and smaller trees in not a very good place, so they do not do so well. They have delicious but small greengage type of fruit, one purple and one green. They all seem to be variable in cropping – some years they get caught by the frost so you get very few, but those that remain are large and juicy. Other years the branches can be overloaded with disastrous results. This happened to the blue plum tree one year when the whole top of the tree collapsed with its burden of not quite ripe fruit. That year, in desperation, we experimented and discovered that not quite ripe plums made good chutney! I have seen several old recipes for pickled plums, but never tried them out. Fruit is amenable to all kinds of experiment if there is a huge surplus, but in these days, when so few people grow their own produce, there are always friends and neighbours to share your excesses.

That tree recovered and became a much easier to pick umbrella shape. All my plum trees need pruning, even if it is only to shorten their fast growing shoots. Do remember to do your pruning before the leaves fall and the sap is down in the late autumn. The Victoria has had minor similar mishaps with smaller, overloaded branches breaking, as I hate thinning out the fruit, always thinking about the quantity ruined by wasps and birds. Quite often, as a result, there are too many small plums, but they go (uncooked) into plastic bags in the freezer for whatever use I feel like putting them to in the winter, while we eat most of the fat juicy ones straight away. I am reminded of a summer holiday in the Scilly Islands in a particularly good plum year when we took a large cooler bag of fruit that made our picnics extra special.

Plums are so good in crumbles, even better than pies. With their strong flavour a really quick dessert would be to make a simple batter, pour over halved plums spread on a baking dish and bake. Think of how good this would be, sprinkled with icing sugar served with a creamy custard. Coming to think of it, plums, like several other fruits would be good in an old fashioned upside down pudding. This is so easy. Just put some stewed fruit in the base of a dish and cover with a simple sponge mix. Cook and turn out and serve with cream or custard.

Plums combine well with other flavours in particular oranges, and go further when put together with apples. Just stewed they are so good with cereal or muesli, with yogurt or cream so I do not bother to do much more with them – although I realise that they would perhaps be enhanced by some liqueur if desired.

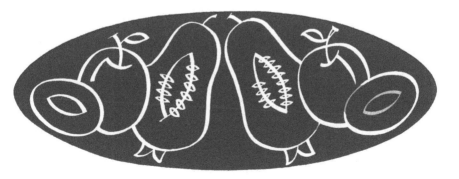

As for jam, any plums will make delicious and easily setting jam. If I had to choose, greengages would be my choice. I have not got a damson tree, but they are quite easy to buy in this part of the world, and make a very different, slightly less sweet, tasting jam than others of the plum family. They set very easily and can become a thick form of preserve often referred to as damson cheese. This can even be cut into small squares, dusted with icing sugar, and served as a confection. Damsons also make a good strong pouring sauce, with or without added liqueur. One difficulty with them is how to get their stones out. A good tip is to freeze the whole fruit for a while because when they defrost they become soft and watery and the stones come out easily.

APPLES

It would be possible to write a whole recipe book based on apples – and probably someone has already done just that. It is best, if you have the space, to have a selection of apples, some cookers and some eaters, preferably ripening at different times. You can always find those grown on small root stock if you have not got much room in your garden. Trees can be trained in cordons or espaliers to go against walls or along a path or behind a flower bed. Then they need careful pruning, but can look wonderful as well as produce a lot of fruit.

We live in a quite ordinary 1920s house which happened to be built in the remains of an old orchard. Most of the almost a hundred year old trees have died, like the greatly missed Cox, but an unnamed green cooker, and a late red eater still survive. In addition we have a fairly early Jonathan which reminds me of the Australian friend who gave me the tree, and prompts me to write to her every year. The best, however, was grown from a seed by my five year old daughter some forty years ago. It has huge pinky yellow almost oval fruit. It is wonderful to eat, or cook and keeps well into early spring. If I knew how to graft shoots I would try to make some more stock from this special tree. I have contacted the apple research unit and they may come over at fruiting time to see whether it is worth their taking some grafts from it. That would be really satisfying.

Apples are my mainstay all the winter and I never tire of stewed apples in one form or another – on their own, with sultanas and perhaps cinnamon, plums, raspberry juice or even combined with a tangerine or satsuma. They can be sweetened with honey or maple syrup for a change from brown or white sugar, and do not need sweetening at all if you include enough sultanas. When I use the word 'stewed' that is not quite accurate because I find that they taste so much better when placed in a pyrex dish and cooked (when there is something else cooking at the same time) in the oven, rather than stewed on top in a saucepan.

As for puddings, where do you start? Pies and flans need no explaining, though I have been far too lazy to create those beautiful glazed arrangements of slices which elevates them into another sphere. Why not try a cobbler for a change, or if you haven't enough time (or cannot be bothered) to roll out the pastry, a crumble. These desserts would look more luscious if you added some red fruit, like Victoria plums or raspberries to colour the juice that often oozes out into the topping.

For family puddings, good old fashioned apple Charlotte, or dumplings in the middle of winter, are hard to beat. However our real family favourite was always a steamed suet pudding like a steak and kidney pudding but with apples inside (plus sultanas or anything else you might like to include, like a plum or two). The suet crust seemed to do something magical to the fruit and juice. I suppose you could make it more sophisticated by including some cider or apple liqueur, but I never bothered. Clotted cream seemed to be the best accompaniment, or home made custard.

The suet pudding's little brother, which you seldom here of today, is apple dumpling. Here suet crust is not absolutely essential, shortcrust would do almost as well. Peel (if you like) and core a large apple or two, stuff them with sultanas or dates (or both), sweeten and fold the pastry round them and bake. I suppose the laziest version is to forget the pastry altogether and just take the stuffed apples, dribble with golden syrup and sit them in a dish with a little water and bake – so simple but so delicious.

Apple Charlotte comes next in its original form and family variations. A standard Charlotte starts with strips of stale bread with butter spread on one side and golden syrup on the other. Filled with cooked apple (plus anything else you like to add), topped with more bread with butter and golden syrup, it is then baked in the oven until brown. Another version can be alternate layers of fruit and toasted bread crumbs. My fastest and laziest version, if you are only one or two people, is this: Fry slices of apple in butter and soft brown sugar. When nearly ready, add small pieces of bread to the delicious sweet buttery juice and fry until nicely crisp and brown.

Apple fritters are a change, those cousins of the delicious banana fritters. Then lovers of batter might enjoy pancakes stuffed with apples, cinnamon or whatever they feel like, smothered with golden syrup, honey, cream or even lemon juice.

That old favourite apple snow should not be forgotten. All it consists of is slightly sweetened sieved stewed apple. Add cream and/or yogurt and perhaps a whisked white of egg. Children love this and it is soothing and comforting for anyone not feeling much like eating. Garnishing it with berries makes it even more enticing.

Apples make a good jelly base for mint, if your mint is still going strong by the autumn. Plain apple jelly is rather bland, nowhere near as good as using the fruit from our two John Downie crab apple trees. These are the large rather pointed cultivated crab apples not the little round hedgerow type. When ripe they are even good to eat (or nibble, to be more accurate, as they are quite small). To my taste, these make absolutely the best jelly, clear, sparkling pink and too delicious to last long. If you leave a fair amount of juice when you are sieving the cooked fruit to make jelly then the remaining pulp makes a very good puree. It is sharper but is a well flavoured alternative to traditional apple snow.

I have not been very successful with making apple juice. Perhaps it is my type of apples but it is usually rather bland to drink. But, do not let this stop you from experimenting, it might be better with the addition of crab apples. Anyhow, you might be more successful than me.

There are plenty of recipes for apple cakes. We used one that went something like this: half a cup of butter, a cup of brown sugar, two cups of cooked apple, cinnamon and/or raisins and an egg I think. I have not made it for a while but remember it was moist and sticky.

There are often more windfalls than can be used at any one time, before they go bad. My solution is to peel, core and cook them (perhaps combined with plums, pears, or even raspberry juice) and pack them into ice cream containers ready to stack in the freezer. Sometimes the windfalls are so small it is a nuisance to peel them, so I just boil them, skin, peel and all and then sieve them. This makes the perfect apple sauce to go later on with pork, and gets frozen in small meal-size containers. This need not be the only use of apples with pork. If chops are going to be grilled or roasted, for example, why not slice some apples alongside to cook in their juices. Apples make excellent chutney with the usual accompaniment of onions and sultanas etc.

Then there are salads. The classic one is apple and celery, but do not be limited by that because chopped or grated dessert apples would enhance so many salads, such as cucumber or carrots. It is up to you to try and dress with your favourite dressing

What about the storage of perfect fruit? I know that the right way is in slatted wooden shelves in your garden shed. That is what my parents did, but the fruit always ended up smelling musty – mice perhaps. Anyhow, I have not got any slatted shelves and my solution works perfectly well. I wrap each apple individually in newspaper, and place in cardboard boxes with the top well fastened down to keep any curious bird or animal from investigating. These just live on the verandah and in most years the contents stay good until Easter. An unheated greenhouse would probably be just as good a place to keep them, but do not think that they need to be kept warm – quite the opposite.

PEARS

I have always envied those who have a walled garden. Pears look so wonderful beautifully trained against the walls, but I suppose they would require pretty skillful pruning. Those of us who are not so lucky must be content with trees in the open. It is a good idea to have one or two varieties if you can. Pears also come on small root stock for small spaces – all the faster to produce fruit too. There is a great deal of difference between the various Williams type dessert pears, some large, some small, and good old fashioned Conference. It is up to you to choose. Some need another tree for the bees to pollinate them, and that is where Conferences are particularly useful. All make delicious eating ripe and raw, and have other possibilities for those who like to experiment.

The classic way which can be found in most recipe books is to poach them in wine and dress up with various toppings. Some people combine different spices with the red wine, such as cinnamon, or vanilla, even cloves, or other flavours such as oranges. You could add your favourite berries to the dish to personalise it. Our favourite way with the large, sweet old fashioned dessert pears whose tree has sadly now died, was this. Cut in half and remove the core leaving a nice depression. Fill this with ice cream and top with hot chocolate sauce. The Conferences are used in a different way. Personally, although they are less attractive in appearance, I think that, when fully ripe, they have the best flavour. However, they cook very well, small or less perfect fruit (such as those visited by the ever voracious wasps) often end up either alone or in my autumn mix of apple, plum and pear, frozen for future use.

I would also try open glazed pear flans which traditionally would be decorated with flaked almonds, although you could try out your own variations – perhaps adding a couple of late peaches. You could experiment with any of the apple ideas, specially the one that fries the fruit in butter and brown sugar before adding small pieces of bread to brown in the mixture. A little wine would then be an optional extra. If you do not want anything so substantial with the bread, forget about it. Just gently fry some not too ripe pears in butter and brown sugar – call them caramelised pears to be fashionable – and enjoy them alone or to accompany almost any special meat dish.

What about quite different uses? When cooking pork chops or a small pork roast I usually roast quartered apples around them, but why not try pears for a change? Pears go well with soft cheeses, especially goats cheese, so you can concoct interesting cold plates dressed with salads. Try watercress or rocket. One day when I had a left-over avocado pear, I experimented with a double pear salad. The crispness of a conference pear went well with the softness of the avocado, dressed with balsamic vinegar. Add some rocket (I leave it to go to seed so it grows all over the garden) or perhaps watercress to make it more decorative. It is up to you to be inventive at times of year when the fruit is plentiful. Why not try pickled pears? They were popular in the days before refrigeration allowed for longer storage.

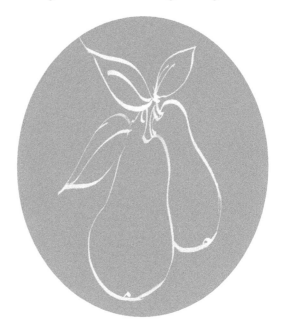

BLUEBERRIES

Depending on what part of the world you live in, blueberries would class as cultivated or wild. Personally, blueberry bushes (despite the illustrations in the glossy advertisement that tempted me to buy them) do not thrive in my garden. Each year they flower but there is not enough fruit to do much with. They just do not like my soil. But holidays in Norway and several other nearer venues have provided large amounts of succulent fruit to eat with cream or experiment with. Somehow, other than these freshly picked ones, i.e. imported bought ones, they often seem better stewed. They combine well with raspberries and other autumn fruit, in any of the ways described, specially in late summer puddings, and, of course, make the traditional blueberry muffins. They also make delicious jam. A completely different use for the juice of stewed blueberries was suggested by an artist friend. She uses it to paint with, and gets various hues of red and blue depending on the consistency.

PEACHES (OR NECTARINES) AND APRICOTS

I have to confess to have been pretty unsuccessful with growing peaches and apricots – but please do not let this put you off, because in the right conditions they thrive, but they need careful pruning. First I tried for several years inside my quite large greenhouse, trying to copy the success of my father in his capacious, old fashioned greenhouse. We got good fruit but in the end were defeated by red spider and I decided that I had better uses for the space. Then, for quite a few years we grew them against the south facing wall of our house, which they need in this country. It is a real thrill growing and picking your own peaches, but eventually it succumbed to something and the space was soon gratefully taken up with our healthy fig tree.

With your own ripe fruit would you really do much except eat them straight off the tree, or give a couple away as a special present – or show them off at the local gardening club? Bought ones yes, treating them much like pears, marinading them and poaching in wine, stuffing them or putting in flans or slicing and setting them in fruit jellies (see page 18). Of course they make a wonderful addition to fruit salads. I suppose there are no real differences between the uses for peaches and nectarines. Personally (though I have never grown them) I prefer nectarines to eat, specially the white fleshed ones. Spiced peaches are delicious too, on their own with ice cream or as an accompaniment to various meat dishes.

As it happens one of my daughters had a small peach and nectarine farm in Western Australia so I had plenty of opportunity to experiment with excess (or parrot pecked) fruit. Peach or nectarine jam is delicious, made in the same proportion with sugar as any other fruit. It is to be found on the menu of most bed and breakfast establishment in W A. I played about with several variations of peach chutney, using the usual mix of onions and sultanas, and vinegar. Stewing them with the plentiful pineapples or apricots was good as would be any tropical fruit – but that is not much help in the south of England, although you might cheat and make them go further with tinned tropical fruit of one sort or another.

As for having my own apricots I was even more unsuccessful. I had always wanted to grow apricots and there are varieties now available that are suitable for our climate. A friend was delighted to find a couple of bare root apricots from somewhere and we both tried hard to get them to prosper – to no avail. If we had found pot grown trees we might have been more successful.

You can find apricots in the shops and with their gorgeous flavour they go a long way, being the ideal stewed fruit to accompany your favourite breakfast cereal, with yogurt. It goes without saying that they make the most wonderful jam, but in this country that would be rather extravagant – but if you buy only a few, they would make a very good upside down pudding and they could be made to go further by combing them with apples.

AUTUMN FRUIT: QUINCES, FIGS AND GRAPES

Two rather different fruits are usually known by the same name – quince. The large-fruited quince tree's Latin name is *Cydonia oblonga*, and the smaller fruited ornamental shrub, commonly called Japonica quince, is *Chaenomeles*. Quinces are usually thought of as a Mediterranean fruit, though originally more widespread, with the ornamental Japonica quince's name pointing to its origin. As far as I can see, the most obvious similarity is their cores. Hard and compact they almost resemble a nut, making it very difficult to cut them up when they are raw. Japonica quinces, as they are called, are small, round and very sour, but add a piquant taste to cooked apples. We have a large Japonica against a south wall which produces beautiful pink blossoms about Easter time, and I hate to waste their fruit so usually make use of some very ripe ones in the autumn – but I would not expect them to be to

everyone's taste. They make a perfectly acceptable jelly. It is nearer in taste to crabapple jelly than the wonderful aromatic larger quince, but perfectly good to eat on toast or to accompany meat or game. Because they tend to be plentiful and perhaps not as flavourful as other autumn jellies, why not use them to experiment a bit. They would be a good vehicle to combine with herbs. Mint would probably be over by then, but lemon thyme or tarragon jelly make interesting accompaniments to meat and game, (even though I doubt if they would come up to my Raspberry and Rosemary Jelly see page 18). But with a good saucepan of jelly you could make small taster pots to see if you like them. All you have to do is to immerse a small bunch of the herb in the hot sweetened juice, leave a while and sieve, before adding a touch of vinegar. I must try borage, my favourite herb next time.

We had a proper quince tree years ago, with large, fat pear-shaped fruit, but sadly its roots succumbed to a fungus disease, and we never got round to planting another. However, a friend down the road has a large tree outside her house and luckily none of the neighbours know what to do with them, so I usually have plenty. The solid quince jelly called marmalata (or marmelo from the Portuguese) is supposed to be the origin of our term, marmalade. Our parents used to bring some back, long ago, from Portugal in big slabs. Now you can often buy it in specialist cheese shops, as it is sold as a good accompaniment for that. We just love the taste in whatever form. Cooked in almost any way that you would treat apples they fill the house with their wonderful aroma. As a preserve you obviously have to peel, core and cook the quinces first. They always seem to come at a busy time of year when there is a lot of other fruit to process, and they are quite difficult to slice and core, although easy to peel. I have found that the easiest way to deal with them is to boil the peeled fruit whole and then the hard core comes out easily in one piece. I freeze containers of the cooked pulp for future use, but enjoy it when freshly cooked, mixed with yogurt or cream, making an unusual dessert. Admittedly preparing them this way it is quite difficult to assess the amount of sugar needed for jam.

You can sieve the cooked pulp with plenty of water for a clear jelly, but to me that always seems rather wasteful and seems to lose a certain amount of the taste. The thick jam made from the whole fruit makes something I consider more delicious. If you are ambitious enough to replicate those slabs of what is usually called quince cheese, then you have to be careful. As you boil it even longer than for jam, it has an annoying tendency to burn, so you have to keep stirring it until it is really thick. Good luck. I know someone who dries slices of quince, and gives them for Christmas – delicious but I have never tried to do it.

FIGS

We have two fig trees growing on south facing walls. Living in the south of England they flourish with us and provide a good harvest most years (for us, birds and wasps). They need pruning, otherwise they would just spread laterally forever. I was taught to restrict each shoot, as it grew in the spring, to four new leaves. You are also advised, when you plant a fig tree to restrict its roots in some way, with a brick box or something similar, or their roots spread and endlessly sprout – think of the huge fig thickets you see growing wild in Mediterranean countries. In very hard winters they can get affected by frost, and will need the blackened tips cutting, but it does not seem to worry the trees too much however hard they have to be cut back.

To be perfect to eat the figs should be starting to split, when they will be juicy and sweet. That is why home grown ones are so much more flavoursome than the perfect looking shop-bought ones. They lend themselves to imaginative uses in salads where they go well halved and topped with soft cheeses. When really plentiful they make an unusual but rather pippy jam, and would make an interesting chutney or relish.

GRAPES

Both of our grape vines have black fruit and are full of seeds. When planted many years ago they were about all that was available. Now, however, there are many white (I always think of them as green) dessert seedless varieties suitable for growing out of doors, though as yet no seedless black grapes, so I am told. Success will depend to a certain extent where you live, and they require a south facing wall to thrive, so you will need to consult a local garden centre or fruit specialist. My grapes need to be fully ripe to be really sweet, and would probably do better if I went around with a pair of scissors and thinned out some of the crowded bunches quite early on. Actually most grapes would profit from this treatment. I have memories of my father, who had several vines rooted outside but growing inside his spacious Victorian greenhouse, continuously thinning to produce perfectly formed bunches.

When some people think of grapes they may only think of wine. I have neither enough of them nor any desire to make wine, but juice is another matter. Mine make delicious juice with a pleasant winey aftertaste. It is even better when combined with the last of the autumn raspberries. Black grapes also make an interesting jelly, although it sometimes is a bit reluctant to set. It might profit from the additional pectin from a few crab apples or japonica quinces, which are plentiful at the same time. Thick and still slightly runny, it is good on ice cream. Having some spare pastry one day, I poured some of it into the case and sprinkled some bread crumbs on top, quite thickly. When baked this made an unusual scrunchy variation of a jam tart somewhat different from my usual way of using left overs when I divide up the pastry case with strips then fill alternate compartments with different jams.

The classic dish that uses dessert grapes in its sauce is *Sole Veronique*. I have never made it but this suggests to me that it might be worth experimenting with seedless grapes and less expensive filleted fish. In addition to uses in ordinary fruit salads, try grapes in salads with cucumber, celery, sliced apples or pears for interesting dressed summer salads.

HEDGEROW FRUITS

ELDERBERRIES AND FLOWERS

These bushes provide the most versatile and delicious of all the wild bounty that can be harvested in our hedgerows. Both flowers and fruit can be used in a variety of ways. I made my own elderflower juice, cordial, syrup or whatever you call it, many years before it became available in expensive supermarkets. Elder bushes grow all over the place in our part of the world. It is best, if possible, not to pick the flowers or fruit right on the side of main roads because of the fumes from cars. The aroma arising from a picked bag or basket of flowers is almost overpowering. For the best results you need to gather the flowers when they are full of pollen – not when they are not quite ready with a hint of green, nor when the pollen is spent and the flowers are beginning to dry up. The trees are most obliging, having a long period of flowering, so you can usually find flowers at the stage that you want.

I trim the bunches and place them in a large bowl with the juice and jest of a couple of good lemons (I usually add the quartered remains as well). Then I cover all this with boiling water, put a clean cloth on top and leave it overnight. The next morning you just need to pass the mix through a sieve. What I do then might not be precisely what you would want to do. Most of the recipes that are around today recommend using quite a lot of citric acid, which in turn means needing adding rather a lot of sugar to the sieved juice. I suppose you would need that to keep the juice from going bad for as long

as possible. However, I do not like the taste of citric acid, and as I freeze most of my juice in small, quickly used up bottles there is no need for other than a tiny bit of it. The amount of sugar they suggest, to counteract the citric acid, I find excessive. I must leave it to individuals to find out what suits their taste and circumstances best.

There are many uses for this delicious concoction. First of all, use it whenever you cook young gooseberries. As described on page 5 it imparts a delicate flavour of muscatel. It adds something extra to a mixed fruit salad, or any cooked fruit like apples or pears. You can make an unusual elderflower water ice which would beguile any dinner party guest, or add some extra lemon juice and try it with a sauce for fish. Then of course drink it. Sparkling water adds an extra element to this drink – but ordinary water is fine. You can add extra lemon, orange or lime to your drink and, of course, adapt the strength to your taste. Decorate it with mint or borage flowers to make it more festive. You could make a jelly of either sort – with gelatin perhaps floating some berries in it, or trying to make a set jelly which would probably need some pectin or the usual accompaniment of gooseberries to help it set.

In spite of the publicity given to commercial elderberry cordial, I have yet to see anyone else gathering the flowers. Quite the reverse – I am often asked what on earth I am doing by passers by when I am out picking.

Now for the fruit. In autumn the same bushes are heavy with clusters of purple berries. They have quite a different flavour and are excellent for jam or, better still, jelly. It is even better when combined with blackberries – either for jelly or to drink. Orange juice enhances their flavours. You need not worry that you are cheating the birds out of food. The harvest is so prolific there is always plenty for everyone.

BLACKBERRIES

No one needs to be told how good blackberries are to eat straight off the bush, and what a perfect family outing blackberrying is on a bright autumn day. But what else can you do with them? You usually get a mix of fat, perfect ones and smaller less good ones. The best are soon gobbled up, although I freeze some of them to go into fruit salads. Then you have a dilemma. Yes, they stew and combine well with apples in any cooked form, but their pips are not to everyone's taste. To puree or juice them is often the best way forward, then you get their flavour combining with the apples or other fruit without the annoyance of pips.

A variation of summer pudding makes a very substantial dessert. You start the usual way by lining a bowl with thinly sliced bread, then fill with layers of fairly thick, sieved blackberries alternating with layers of bread until the bowl is full. Make sure to keep back enough juice to ensure each layer of fruit and bread is well moistened so no bread, outside or in, remains uncoloured

It goes without saying that it is worth freezing bottles of juice, whether blackberry alone or combined with whatever else is around at the time. Ice cream or blackberry and apple fool, as creamy as you wish, is always welcome. Blackberry jelly is so simple, just cook and sieve and add sugar and it sets easily.

DAMSONS AND SLOES

Like some other fruits, damsons can be classed as either cultivated or hedgerow fruit. Those that grow wild, particularly in the West Country, are bushes or trees that usually look smaller and less impressive than their better looked-after, cultivated cousins. The fruit tends to be sourer and smaller too, but just as suitable for stewing, jam or cheese, as the thick conserve is sometimes called, and including in pies mixed with apple if you wish. When sieved, the pulp can be used to make another slightly different summer pudding, with alternate layers of pureed fruit and thin slices or bread as described with blackberries on page 15. As mentioned earlier, stoning the fruit can be tiresome and time consuming. Unexpected stones in jams or pies can be disastrous for your teeth but there is an easy way of dealing with them. Just freeze your sloes for a short while and when they thaw they become soft and the stones are easier to extricate.

Sloes are quite a different matter with their much smaller purple fruit they are so often ignored by passers by. Their traditional use is for making sloe gin. Just prick the fruit and pack in a bottle or jar with plenty of sugar – then cover generously with gin. Shake occasionally and leave it at least six months before drinking. One autumn we were taking a Canadian colleague around Kent and parked near a stately home in the Weald. There was a hedge completely covered in sloes. He was very excited as he had been born in Estonia and he remembered the fruit from his childhood. We never got inside the stately home but spent the time picking sloes. I have always thought that sloes made a wonderful, very strong pouring sauce, but this crop had to be made into jelly in order to travel back in the plane. That was equally good. Sadly, the hedge was destroyed shortly after in order to enlarge the car park, but luckily I know of several other good sites.

ROSEHIPS

During the Second World War everyone was encouraged to harvest and use rosehips as the ideal form of free vitamin C. I was at school then, but bottles of rosehip syrup were provided for all young children by the health clinics. Similar bottles were sold in chemist shops for several years after the war, but this delicious drink has long been forgotten. To be honest it is quite a job to extract the full flavour of rose hips.

You can just simply boil them for quite a long time and pour off the resulting juice – but that loses a lot of the goodness. The next stage, however, is to split open the now softened hips and extract the thistly sort of centre from each one. Then when you re-cook the fruit you get the full goodness of the flesh inside, and the resulting juice, when you sieve the mix, is thicker and usually bright pink. Now you can sweeten it and bottle it ready to drink, or go right ahead and add more sugar and produce a wonderful jelly It is well worth the trouble. It is worth mentioning that there is a species of cultivated rose, that is advertised as good for making prickly hedges, also good for making syrup, wine and jelly.

CRAB APPLES

Wild crab apples are often to be found in hedgerows and elsewhere. In fact, in autumn I can see one in my neighbour's garden with its small red fruit just being left for the birds which is a bit of a waste. Whereas you can eat the cultivated ones when ripe, see page 29, I would not try to eat the wild ones raw as they remain pretty sour, but are very good for making jelly.

You can try other berries if you first make quite sure that they are meant to be eaten. Constance Spry mentions a jelly of hips and haws, although I would prefer to stick to hips alone. I once tried to make a jelly out of Rowan (*Sorbus*) berries, which are prolific in Scotland, and recommended as good to eat with game, but I found them far too bitter. In past generations it was essential for country folk to pickle and preserve everything they could to last them through the long winter. I liked Mrs Beeton's remark, a hundred years and more ago: 'When fruit and vegetables are cheap – cheap enough to pickle – it is the duty of the economical mistress to preserve and pickle. Not unpleasant work is it either'. It is not a duty any more, and with freezers to help us it is even more of a pleasure to harvest and preserve the good things in the hedgerows as well as our own garden produce.

THE GREEN GREENHOUSE

And what it can produce

The wonderful greenhouse was a major factor in why we purchased our not very spectacular 1920s house, some fifty years ago. Most people would have converted it into a luxurious sun room, long ago. Built on to the house, it has doors from the veranda and into the garden, and one way or another provides us with food nearly all the year round, and a lot of pleasure as well. Originally, when we had a solid fuel boiler that my poor husband had to stoke morning and evening before and after work, it was heated by enormous lead pipes. When we fitted a gas boiler it no longer made economic sense to go on heating it – we had to revise our plans a bit, but have never really missed the heat. We started off with grand ideas of having a grapevine, but we soon found a vine did quite well outside. Then I tried a peach but that never really prospered and attracted red spiders etc. It also did perfectly well outside against a south facing wall. Slowly I found other and better uses for the space.

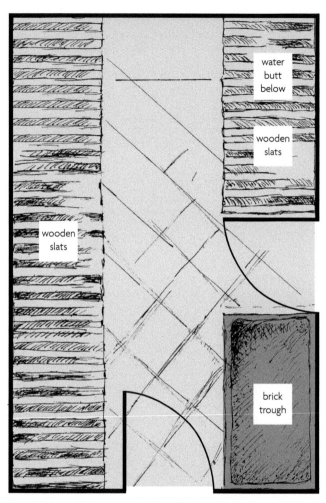

The greenhouse measures approximately 14ft by 9ft. It has two doors, one opening off the veranda and one opening into the garden. The left side consists entirely of a waist high slatted surface, while the right side has an invaluable brick sided trough for half the length. The other half is slatted with a water butt underneath it, fed from the roof. The floor is tiled except for a small section of bare earth at the far end.

It would be hard to say what is my favourite time of the year in my greenhouse. Is it when the first green sprouts appear in the spring, or a little later when seedlings are planted out in serried ranks in their boxes? Is it when the tomato plants are neatly settled in their final home or when the whole greenhouse is aglow with tomatoes and multicoloured peppers? Anyhow, throughout the year, it is the place where I relax and recover from the hassles of daily life.

Before starting on the calendar year let me explain how I have worked things out to make things simple and recycle all I can. The experts surely would not approve of many of my methods but it all works for me, costs very little and does no harm to the environment.

This is how I circulate the soil in the greenhouse. The soil comes straight from my overflowing compost heaps. It gets used in the trough, boxes and pots for tomatoes, peppers and cucumbers etc. The next spring it is sieved and used for planting seeds (the tomatoes get used cucumber soil). My seeds get planted in various smallish sized polystyrene boxes that come from my travelling fishmonger. He says that he has to pay to dispose of them so it is doing him a favour! Later on larger, salmon-sized boxes house my tomatoes. Perhaps here is the place to mention that as I get older many of the things I do are designed to make life easier as well.

I start in late January or early February depending on the weather. There is not much good starting too early when we are snowed and frozen up as we have been in several years. The first edible crops that I plant are quick greenhouse salads. I sprinkle seeds of quick growing leaf salads of various kinds in the large pots that had housed cucumbers. They can be covered up for a few days if the weather outside is truly awful, and then may take a little longer than the advertised fortnight to develop. Into the trough that was home to tomatoes I plant sprouting peas which make delicious salad and go well with the first sprouting mint which will soon be emerging outside, The pea sprouts will go on until I need the space for my tomatoes. Also an early crop of spinach is a welcome addition and so easy to grow. An old washing up bowl would be quite an acceptable receptacle for this, and it is so much easier to pick the delicious small leaves at waist height rather than bending down to harvest them.

I should explain that, because of the multitude of pesky wildlife – pigeons, mice, foxes and I don't know what else, that think my garden is their private larder, I have to start all my vegetable seedlings in the greenhouse. The first seeds that are planted are broad beans and then the first lot of Little Gem, those delicious small cos lettuces. Leeks are next, followed by beetroot and spinach beet. Over the years I have abandoned brassicas, (whose seeds would have been planted soon, one by one). My soil had never really suited them, and

they became more and more difficult to protect from the pigeons. The last straw was when, in several bad winters, snow weighted down my nets and broke my precious sprouting broccoli. Other people may have different vegetables that they would plant and plan accordingly. This is not meant to be about outdoor vegetables but they tend to creep in somehow.

Back to the greenhouse – the broad beans are ready to plant out in no time, and the first lettuces are ready to prick out into boxes, and leeks are soon ready to plant outside. We are on light, sandy soil which soon dries out in a hot spring, so I like to get anything hardy out quite early. Then it is time to get out my small propagator. I used to have an electric one but when it no longer worked, I found that my daughter's discarded ordinary one does just as well. It has two small compartments, one each for my two favourite varieties of tomatoes – Alicante and Gardeners Delight. I have experimented with various other varieties, yellow ones, striped ones, etc over the years but as these two seem to work well for me I don't bother with any others these days. The little seedlings will need planting out into boxes and growing on before being ready for their permanent homes. Then when the plants look large and strong enough they get put straight into their permanent homes. (If they were going to be planted out of doors they would need to be potted up and grown on a third time). Three Alicante plants go into each large polystyrene box that my fishmonger friend told me once housed salmon. Six Gardener's Delight go into the trough, with a further three into a box on the floor. The plants of the larger tomatoes will be limited to three trusses each. They sit on the slatted shelf and would be quite difficult to control any higher, and this way the yield, in a relatively small space, is maximised. On the other hand, the smaller cherry type tomatoes are allowed to grow to six trusses, and perhaps even more towards the end of the season when unobserved shoots grow upwards and prolong the season. The only feed they get is one bottle of seaweed fertiliser between them all, applied when they start to form small fruit.

Then it is time to pop in my two varieties of pepper seeds. They need slightly more heat to get them started. Eventually, having been transplanted to grow stronger, they go, three at a

time into smaller polystyrene boxes. Whether or not they would do better separately in large pots is immaterial – there just would not be enough space for them all. My way I get about five peppers from each plant therefore, between the six or seven boxes there are plenty to go around. They need little care other than watering and some short stakes if they grow too tall.

Now I must confess some of my other sins or if you prefer, economies. I do buy my tomato seeds even though plenty of seedlings seem to appear in the compost somehow. However, as many other seeds as possible I keep and store each year to use again. Let us start with peppers. Some twenty years ago, just after the Russians left Hungary, I went to a conference in Budapest. We drove there instead of flying. There was little to buy in the shops in those days, but on the way back the roadside was littered with piles of grapes, plums and peppers for sale. The sweet red peppers looked like overgrown carrots and the yellow ones were quite small and slightly blunter, but neither were like anything we had seen – before or after – in shops. We ate the grapes and plums and also the peppers, but I kept their seeds and have been growing them annually ever since. These peppers always produce a good crop, and they stack conveniently like ice cream cones for freezing.

The other peppers that I have grown now for three of four years I acquired in a quite different way. I supervised a Ph D student whose wife was obviously a keen gardener, because one day he came bearing an unusual gift. It consisted of two huge, almost round peppers with strange, indented sides. They were so beautiful it almost seemed a crime to eat them.

Needless to say I kept the seeds. The next year they fruited prolifically but we had so many and they obviously were not the right shape for freezing so we got rather tired of them. That was lucky, because, left longer until the plants began to look quite tired, the peppers unexpectedly turned bright yellow. Then they were so sweet that no way were any wasted. They worked well both cooked or stuffed and were delicious cut up raw in salads.

I keep some seeds of all the different varieties of beans – broad, runner and climbing french. Some get used for cooking but there are always plenty left. Runner bean beans (they profit from being immersed in water overnight) are particularly good cooked with a boiled bacon joint, along with onions, leeks and carrots, plus a few lentils. Even corn is kept and stored and kept for future use if I let a cob get over ripe and dry. My first storage system consisted of a display rack used for the confectionery Tic Tac. I spotted it somewhere, about to be discarded. It held about twenty transparent plastic packs, with fitted tops and did very well for many years, and took up very little room. As my store of seeds expanded it has been supplemented with various pots. It is an added pleasure that there are usually plenty of seeds to share with friends.

You always read that it is desirable to have a glass frame to accustom your seedlings to the cruel outside world before planting them out. There was one when we first arrived, against the south wall of our greenhouse. It was huge and heavy, but I persevered in the days when I followed rules – until the time that the whole edifice collapsed. Luckily it was in a very sheltered corner with another wall that gives protection from the east wind. Now only the solid base remains, so boxes of seedlings may, if I am very energetic, bask there for a few days. Then that space is filled with more good compost-filled boxes. Apart from being an ideal place for herbs, it is lovely to have a few things for when I do not want to go right up the garden. I look on it as an extension to my greenhouse. Lettuces do well there, a few spinach beet sometimes do better than up the garden, half a dozen climbing French beans are conveniently near my back door and this year I am trying something new. I saw on a gardening programme, that if you plant carrots up high enough, the carrot flies (the bane of my garden) cannot reach them. They are supposed to fly only about eighteen inches from the ground. So I have a tall, square box standing on a base and hope for the best. A bucket would do just as well.

The cucumber seeds get planted at the beginning of April. I grow an unusual variety of mini ones that seem to work well. They have never prospered outside but do not like too much heat and tend to have a fairly short, though prolific, fruiting period. The first two largest seedlings go into a very spacious pot and seem not to mind being together. The next two go singly into slightly smaller pots and go out into my sheltered sunny corner as soon as the weather is warm enough. They will be brought in as their older siblings are starting to fade. A final couple will be planted outside in a box, where they will never fruit. They will be carefully dug up when finally needed. Of course, I could phase out the planting of the seeds, but somehow my enthusiasm for planting and pricking out seeds wanes as the space gets filled with growing tomatoes. By the time the cucumbers are in their final pots, corn, courgettes, pumpkins and late beans are all vying for space and attention. There are often extras around and any extra seedlings find willing homes with friends. It is a good way of keeping everyone happy – me because my orphans find happy homes, and other people who are often encouraged to try growing their own, sometimes for the first time. It sounds as if all this is a lot of work, but most jobs get fitted in odd moments, except for the emptying of all the containers of used soil, sifting whatever is suitable to use for planting seeds, then chucking what is left onto the shrubbery or elsewhere.

There is no good pretending that the care of greenhouse crops is a quick job, but it is so satisfying. If my greenhouse were at the bottom of the garden, instead of right off my veranda, perhaps it would all be more time and energy consuming. People seem to be amazed to see that it is possible to grow successful crops, in boxes with just home-made compost. It takes a certain amount of attention and care to achieve this. The tomato plants need examining every few days to take out any rogue side shoots that develop at amazing speed if left undetected and take useful sustenance away from the plant. Then they need careful tying up to their supporting canes as they grow. They need watering every day, sometimes more in very hot weather – to their roots if possible rather than the lazier way of swishing all over with a hose. Rain water from the tank is best, but this has to be supplemented sometimes in dry periods with mains water. My greenhouse water tank, that drains rain water off the roof, is essential, for ease as much as economy or green considerations in our part of the country where hosepipe bans are not unknown.

Cucumbers are not so easy for me to grow in my greenhouse. Nor do they produce too much from each plant. They tend to dry up after a while in hot seasons. Cucumbers (like all of their relations – pumpkins, etc) fruit best on side shoots. You have to be cruel and keep on taking out the tops, starting with the main growth. You have to be careful not to let them fruit too low down on the stem, or this weakens the plant. It hurts me to curtail them this way, but the benefits soon show when the side shoots prosper and soon present me with miniature cucumbers adorned with a flower bud. I tend to shorten those side shoots as soon as they reveal that miniature fruit. Cucumbers need lots of thin canes to climb up, and their wandering tendrils sometimes need a bit of encouragement to find an anchor.

HERBS

The only herbs that I grow regularly in the greenhouse are basil and parsley. That is not because I do not use more, but all the others (including coriander) seem to grow quite happily outside. If I forget to plant the basil or parsley seeds in time, I can always be lazy and buy some at my local supermarket. In that case I divide up the plants into two or three pots when I get home as they are always too crowded. All the basil stays in the greenhouse, but the parsley is divided between indoors and out. Some years one lot does better throughout the winter outside than inside – sometimes the other way round.

USING MY GREENHOUSE PRODUCE

The main purpose is obviously to have fresh produce for as long as I can extend the growing season. I can often manage to have a few tomatoes up until December by picking and storing the last green ones in a bowl before uprooting the plants. There are usually gluts, particularly in mid-season and that is where the freezer comes into its own. All during the season the fattest of my Gardener's Delight tomatoes get picked and frozen in large plastic bags, along with sprigs of basil. Any excess, larger Alicante plants are cooked and sieved to be frozen as soup or juice before they get over-ripe. Left whole, I do not think they would freeze too well. The Hungarian peppers are so convenient. They just stack together in small freezer bags. I have not had a surplus of the large yellow ones yet, but I suppose I could cut them up, ready to use, and freeze them that way – or as my friends often say – buy another freezer, but where to put it?

Cucumbers would not freeze but if there are plenty, they make my favourite pickle – but more of that in the next section. I should mention that I have grown aubergines quite successfully in the greenhouse in the past, but they were not very popular with the family. All that remains to be said is that the greenhouse needs a thorough clear out in early winter, ready for the next year.

USING TOMATOES AND PEPPERS

Those small Gardener's Delight tomatoes are so delicious, picked and eaten straight away or served whole in a salad, that it is surprising any remain to be frozen and stored. However they produce prodigious amounts so I can easily pick the largest ones to save as they appear. This is not meant to be a whole list of recipes. Everyone will have different produce saved, and probably have their own ideas of how to use it. So here are just a few ideas of how I use my frozen tomatoes and peppers. There is no good pretending that the small frozen tomatoes taste the same as fresh ones, or that they can be eaten other than cooked, but they are incredibly

useful in so many ways. Another thing that it is fair to mention is that you end up with quite a lot of skins. However these come off very easily once they begin to unfreeze in the pan. Just pinch them and the whole skin comes off in one and empties out its contents.

An easy way is to use them in scrambled eggs or to cook with ingredients such as liver and bacon or sausages where they contribute to a flavoursome sauce. For any kind of risotto or pasta dish start with up to a dozen tomatoes and a couple of peppers adding any herbs you might wish. Add to them a couple of onions which I dry well and then string up in the larder. They are not as grand as the ones that Breton farmers used to bring around on their bicycles, but this way they last all through the winter and taste really strong, unlike supermarket ones that taste of little and have an annoying tendency to go bad. Onions and shallots are so easy to grow – just plant the sets out early in the spring and leave them to grow.

One of our favourite dishes is a squid stew, which starts with the usual mixture of tomato, peppers and onion (fennel or dill are good additions). This concoction can have any other shell fish in it, for instance prawns or mussels. You could also include white fish if you like. The sauce that results from this mix of flavours is truly delicious, and with a dash of cream it rivals any restaurant dish. Peppers alone enhance any curry or stew, and without any accompanying tomatoes, their own particular flavour comes out more strongly.

The larger tomatoes do not have quite the same taste as the small ones. They are ideal for slicing and putting into salads with whatever else you like, and best with a good dressing. They are good halved and grilled, stuffed or not, but you will not need ideas for how to use them those ways. As I have said, I would not freeze the larger tomatoes whole. They would be very watery. They have a tendency to get over ripe late in the season, then they split and quickly go bad, so you need to keep an eye on them. To store them they should be cooked with a minimum of water – just enough to keep them from sticking to the pan – and then sieved to remove seeds and skins.

Watching a smart cooking programme I learned that the thin, light coloured liquid that comes through the sieve first has most of the flavour and is much prized, however I prefer mine to be thicker and bright red! At one stage I experimented with making a sort of ketchup/tomato sauce, but anyhow once the juice is frozen you could do anything you want with it later on. Writing all this down makes me think around the subject. It might be good idea for me (or you) to fill some little pots as well as the usual larger soup containers. Then there would be just the right amount to add what you want to it to make a quick tomato sauce. It is of course just like the very best tomato juice, when served cold.

I choose, however, to use it for a variety of soups, either on its own or combined with other vegetables, leeks, Jerusalem artichokes and, best of all, butternut squash. These friendly plants spread themselves happily over any space left in the garden by early vegetables like broad beans, or even onions or early potatoes which are usually harvested before the squashes really expand. Apart from helping to keep weeds down, they keep for months which make them very useful in the winter. Back to soups: I would usually finish them off with a swirl of yogurt on top, and then, depending on what is around at the time, either cut a mix of herbs on top of that or toast some pine nuts. Like so many other dishes, this can be defrosted quickly and served in no time to any unexpected guest.

Of course there are other uses for tomatoes. You can concoct various chutneys with them, either red or green. Green chutneys suit those who grow their tomatoes outside where so many fail to ripen. I have made it years ago but must confess to not liking it very much.

USING CUCUMBERS

The trouble with these small cucumbers is that they are so delicious raw that not many are left to experiment with. This would not happen with full-sized ones, but my little ones tempt anyone venturing into the greenhouse to pluck one and eat it whole, just like an apple. Of course plenty survive to become salad ingredients, either sliced on their own, or mixed with tomatoes, etc and finished off with an oil and vinegar dressing. When fed up with cucumbers alone and unadorned there are plenty of other dressings to enhance them like dill with mayonnaise or yogurt. This is particularly good with smoked salmon.

It has to be a bumper crop to enable me to make my favourite pickle. (I should add that the climate has an effect on the yield – too hot and the plants quickly shrivel up, and in really cold springs the seeds are difficult to germinate and the few resulting plants never produce very heavy crops.) I have looked at various recipes for it but just adapted them for what I have in store. Having sliced the cucumbers thinly, onions and lots of dill seed goes in. (Dill seeds itself annually all over my garden, as does rocket.) A green pepper would be a good addition, but mine are unlikely to be ready in time. You could add turmeric or mustard seed, if you like, as suggested in some recipes, not forgetting brown sugar. One year I was given some very strong Swedish vinegar (it had to be diluted) and that imparted a particularly interesting flavour.

Now, all through the writing of this book, I have been offered ideas from friends and colleagues. Although over the years maybe I have adapted some of other people's ideas, I have not included anything here that I have not tried myself. I would really like to copy the great Mrs Beeton who invited the readers of her original cookery articles to contribute their own ideas. It is said that many of these ideas found their way into her final books – but that will have to wait for another day.

THE VEGETABLE GARDEN

Changing priorities over fifty years

This part of the book is slightly different. A vegetable garden is dependent on so many factors. Firstly what are your tastes, how big is your plot, what your soil is like and finally but perhaps the most important, what size and age is your family? All that I can offer as a general guide, is how we coped with all these variables.

When we came to this garden, over fifty years ago, I already had experience in starting up instant vegetable gardens – two of them during three years in East Africa, and two in another three years in Yorkshire. In Uganda it was easy, everything grew in double quick time, even when moving around we could get crops of beans, corn, carrots and plenty of salad crops – and strawberries of course. (We also just managed a hand of bananas from two trees that we had actually planted but we did not stay long enough for our pineapples to grow from the tops of ones we had eaten and popped back into the soil.) Yorkshire was colder and in smaller plots it was mostly beans and salads in the summer and brussels sprouts in the winter. When we arrived in Kent, not surprisingly, we hoped it would be more permanent though perhaps did not anticipate that we would still be here fifty years later!

WITH YOUNG CHILDREN

When we first started this garden we had two small children and another arrived shortly afterwards. There was not much time or energy to devote to vegetables. It had, however, always been a tradition in the family to produce as much as possible so I did my best. Anyhow there was a need to cover the large beds or they would just become weed patches.

Looking back, conditions were very different in those days. I cannot remember any serious problems with slugs or pigeons destroying my vegetable crops. On the other hand there were more small birds around like thrushes to consume my fruit so netting was needed there. I had no worries about carrot fly or club root with my brassicas. I was able to pop seeds straight into the ground, carrots, spinach beet, broad and French beans etc and usually they grew quite well with no further care. Marrows helped to cover the ground (it was before courgettes were generally available). Maybe I transplanted salad crops but maybe I just scattered seeds and then thinned them out.

I did not do much in the greenhouse at first and was not at all ashamed to buy small plants from local nurseries when I saw them. If I remember correctly, that is where I got my brussels sprouts and sometimes cauliflowers. It was before the days of freezers and everything was consumed as soon as it was picked, and very simply steamed or cooked quickly by other methods – so, sorry, not many recipes.

Then I thought of those things that were perennial and would need least care and attention. It may seem strange, but almost the first thing I did was to plant a large asparagus bed. Asparagus crowns are easily obtainable, so all you have to do is to spread their roots, cover them and wait a year or maybe two for them to be ready to be cut. The general rule is to harvest them during May and the first half of June and then leave the stalks to grow to strengthen the plant for the next year. My bed was to last at least 30 years, and by the time it was exhausted several patches of self-seeded plants were thriving (and still are).

Then, probably borrowing from my parents' garden, came the two sorts of artichokes – Jerusalem and Globe. Luckily the Jerusalem artichokes were planted in a far corner, because once established they become impossible to get rid of. They still inhabit that same corner after 50 years, and unchanged soil does not seem to worry them! When you dig up a clump in the winter, keep the largest potato-like products, or whatever you call them, and leave a couple of small ones to come up the next year. Anyhow, with the most careful harvesting, some will always remain hidden in the soil, so you never would get rid of them. We have always loved these artichokes – in soups, (particularly accompanied by leeks and any other root vegetable or butternut squash and any stock around) roasted with potatoes, curried with carrots and other left over vegetables or covered with a strong cheese sauce. Few people seem to appreciate them these days and I have some difficulty in giving away any surplus. People seem to associate them with tiresome, lumpy things, difficult to peel. The secret is to be sure to dig them all up thoroughly each spring. Take out all the large ones, because it is those that grow lumps on their surface the next season. This way you are assured of lump-free artichokes that are as easy to peel as potatoes. The name Jerusalem artichoke is supposed to come from the French word girasol, that means sunflower. They are, in fact, a form of sunflower, but it has to be a very hot summer for them to produce their pitifully small flowers on the top of their very tall stalks.

Globe artichokes are quite different. With their beautiful foliage, and if you choose to leave them instead of eating them, their giant thistle-like flowers, they can just as easily be grown in the flower border. Wherever you plant them they just increase their clumps, year-by-year and let you take root cutting in the spring to give away. This is just as well, because mine eventually succumbed in an extremely cold winter and there were friends to supply new cuttings from my old plants, to start again.

As for cooking, I have never done anything other than just boil and eat them, leaf by leaf with the expectation of the delicious heart as your reward (once you have removed the prickly choke that gives them their name). If you want a quantity of artichoke hearts for some special dish I think it is better to buy them in tins.

WITH A GROWING FAMILY

Children grow and so do their appetites. First comes nursery school and eventually full time school. At last there is a bit more time (and need) to do more in the vegetable garden. The greenhouse began to come into its own and I could start off my seeds and seedlings earlier. There was still a heavy glass frame just outside the greenhouse that made things even easier, spoiling the seedlings with a few days of acclimatisation before being planted out. Eventually it collapsed of old age and never was replaced. Seedlings seem to have survived quite well being transplanted straight out into the garden ever since.

The soil had been in pretty good condition when we arrived and I do not suppose I did much to improve it during those early years except perhaps composting a trench for some hungry crop. Now, however, the sandy soil needed a bit of replenishing. There was plenty of well-rotted manure available in those days, delivered from local farms. I used a lot of energy carting it up the long garden path in an ancient wheelbarrow.

Compost was (and still is) kept in several compartments at the end of the garden, and what was not used to replenish greenhouse containers was spread around. I did not use chemicals at all. If my lettuces, or other plantlets, were threatened by wandering slugs, then there was plenty of soot from the chimney sweep to sprinkle round to protect them.

What changed in my planting regime? For one thing I stopped growing ordinary French beans and changed to ones that climbed like runners. They yielded far more and were so much easier to pick. Two plantings of runner beans a year, climbing up teepees made of bamboo canes grown in the garden, extended their season. As well as eating them young we have always been fond of the actual beans. You always find some that you have left too long and have grown too tough to eat. The pods end up drying at the end of the season and make a welcome addition to winter stews. They are particularly good with boiled bacon joints, along with onions and other root vegetables (and perhaps some lentils). You may need to soak the beans over night if they have got too dry.

Perhaps it is time to mention again my habit of keeping plenty of seeds to plant the next year. Beans are an obvious choice and I have not needed to buy any for many years.

What had not altered was our liking of broad beans. They now demanded two plantings to make sure we had enough. When we finally got a freezer we found that if there was a glut, broad beans they froze very successfully. They just need blanching in boiling water for minute or two, and then are ready to put into bags and freeze. I cannot say the same for runner beans. They do not freeze well, but my climbing French ones are firmer and are just about edible when defrosted.

I remember how the children loved podding peas so I suppose we must have grown them in the days before pigeons. There must have been a couple of rows to satisfy all our appetites.

There was a great expansion of brassicas even though some plants had a tendency to suffer from club root and needed more lime. Of course we continued with plenty of sprouts. There is something special about going out on Christmas morning and gathering them to go with the turkey, even in the snow. We found curly kale popular and prolific, but best of all we enjoyed sprouting broccoli in the spring, both purple and white. We went on to grow them until quite recently until defeated by pigeons and snow. What happened was that voracious pigeons attacked them whenever they could, even through netting. The winter snow added to the problems by weighing down the netting and damaging, even breaking the tops of the plants. I miss them every spring, as those that you can buy in shops taste of nothing.

I never seriously grew cabbages. They were so easily available and tricky to grow, particularly red ones. We have always enjoyed red cabbage, cut up with apples, onions and sultanas, with some brown sugar and casseroled in the oven for a couple of hours.

Even when courgettes became available marrows were still a good idea as well, as the children enjoyed stuffed marrow (providing they were not too large when they became tasteless). Tomatoes were now in the greenhouse, free from mildew, and two varieties of lettuces were grown in succession as seedlings until I finally decided that several plantings of Little Gems suited us best.

When there was enough space, I grew first early potatoes, but have never bothered with main crop ones. There was never any need to grow onions in those days. Breton onion sellers turned up regularly every autumn with their braids of onions which would last us through the winter and longer. They also made good Christmas presents for town dwelling friends and relations.

At about that time we were given a clump of perpetual spring onions. They have multiplied and grown into an oft-moved row, edging the path. They are incredibly useful for salads when fresh and plump, before they begin to separate once more. later in the summer. Their greenery can be used in cooking at any time that you need a little oniony flavour. In our family they are known as His Excellency's onions as they came from the garden of someone who had once been an ambassador. I have never seen them advertised in a catalogue but they must be available somewhere. Needless to say there are plenty of their descendants in friends' gardens today.

Leeks came fairly soon, also started in the greenhouse. A row does not take up much space, and they look after themselves and are so valuable in the winter. You can eat the best white parts, just as they are or in a cheese sauce, boil the tops and use as a basis for soups, with potato and artichoke, or whatever you like.

Of course I kept up carrots and parsnips. There is something about carrots that fascinates children. I noticed it first with my three, and later with my grandchildren. Pulling them up and finding what was growing underneath was a never-ending source of excitement.

Perhaps I should add that, long before the children went to school, they had their own little patches to tend. They had carrots, lettuces radishes and perhaps a couple of strawberry plants, maybe even a tomato. Their enthusiasm might not have lasted then for very many years but the habit stuck. Now with their own children, wherever they are in the world, they grow as much as possible of their own produce.

Just as we adults find gardening therapeutic, so do children. I think that the following is worth recording. My youngest child contracted a condition that confined her to bed for over a year. We fixed her up a little garden by her bed, constructed of egg boxes where she enjoyed watching

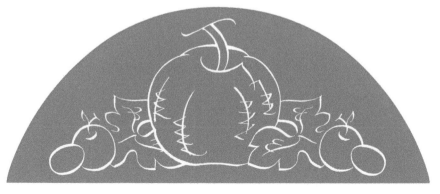

mustard and cress and other similar sprouting plants grow —
and then eating them.

My aim had been to provide vegetables for the family all
year round, and we more or less succeeded. But I repeat, what
you grow depends on what your family likes and will eat, and
that probably varies from family to family.

THE EMPTYING NEST

There is an amazing surge of energy when the last son or
daughter finally leaves the home. As far as the garden is
concerned it allowed us to experiment and grow different
things. Let me say that gardening has never been the only way
I spend my time. I have always carried on with my design
work, as well as writing and research. Yet planning, and
carrying out those garden plans, is as creative as any of my
other activities. The attitude of other people has always
amused me. 'It is all right for you', they would say, 'You have
green fingers', as if it were a disease or some heredity defect.
Personally. I have always found gardening the most relaxing
and satisfying of occupations.

Anyhow, how did things change? Certainly no more
marrows, but different types of courgettes, yellow and dark
took their place. Butternut squash, and Australian firm, small
pumpkins were introduced. These are amazing vegetables, so
easy to grow and after harvesting will keep for months, right
into the spring. You can roast them, mash them with potato,
add cubes to stews and, best of all, make wonderful,
sustaining soups. I did not find the Halloween type pumpkins
to have as much taste so never grew them. We went back to

growing spinach beet, one of the few vegetables that the children did not like. We tend to separate the stem from the leaf part. That is because I think the stem is the best part, worthy of being eaten on its own – while my husband prefers his spinach green.

Now there are multicoloured types of spinach beet, that look as much at home in the flower border as the vegetable patch.

The Bretons have long gone so onions and shallots now go in early on in the year. I am always amazed how the smallest home-grown onion has enough flavour to do the job of several large, tasteless, bought ones. I dry them a bit when harvested, then hang them in the larder in braided strings. They are not as large as the French ones but last through the winter and taste wonderful. Shallots impart a sweeter flavour (in the years when they grow well, otherwise they are rather fiddly to deal with). Then peas. A friend introduced me to a variety of climbing peas called, I think, Aldenham. They were incredible, with enormous pods and still the same delicious flavour. I grew them for quite a few years, always saving a few seeds for the following year, until pigeons made it quite impossible to protect them.

Throughout the years, people have suggested that I should put permanent netting over the whole garden, but it has never seemed worthwhile. Even to do part of it would cause problems as rotation of crops is essential long term. This was brought home to me several years ago, when I had grown runner beans in the same location for several years. It was because I had a convenient wire contraption there that worked well. After a few years the plants did not do well, the leaves had a blackish tinge and I had learned my lesson. Now, like most other vegetables, they have a different location each year.

Corn became a favourite crop, again because the flavour is so wonderful compared with anything found in the shops. It was so easy to grow, and a joy to watch. All you had to do was to make sure the plants were grown quite close together in order to fertilise each other. This went well for quite a long time until suddenly tragedy struck. The ready-to-harvest plants were found flat on the ground, and the golden cobs all chewed up. At first I suspected badgers, as one had taken up residence in a nearby garden and was causing havoc. It succumbed to the traffic on our busy road, therefore, when it happened the next year I came to the conclusion that the foxes that roamed the neighbourhood must be guilty. If I wanted to preserve my corn I had to build a substantial barricade around them. It rather takes the fun out of things.

Not everything I tried was a success, I never managed to grow celery and my beetroot remained stubbornly small. Fluctuations in the weather has influenced the size and quality of some crops, but that is the reality of gardening.

GARDENING AS YOU GET OLDER

Then you get older, or something else occurs to focus your mind on the necessity of making things easier. With me it was a stroke at the age of 68. The greenhouse was always accessible but not much else during the wheelchair months. I soon discovered that a garden fork was a much better support than a stick, and plastic chairs placed conveniently up the path made good resting places. Several years later I discovered a four-wheeled walker that made life even easier. I could store things under the seat and then rest on it as needed. My bucket, that was often full and heavy, sat on that seat when I did not. However it is not just a matter of walking aids. Gardening can play a huge amount in a recovery, providing motivation to get up in the morning as well as vital exercise.

Enough of that, what about actual garden planning that would probably have much wider implications? I soon discovered the desirability of growing more on the edges of the beds, easier to plant up and later to weed and gather. This left the centre of the beds free to let pumpkins and squashes wander at will. Bean poles could still go anywhere and provided good support for me as well as the crop. I found that it was necessary to keep plants further apart, so I did not squash anything, being rather more unsteady on my feet, as many elderly gardeners might be.

Now, I know that it is fashionable to promote raised compartments on larger area of garden. It might, after a lot of work, make life easier. This method of gardening certainly looks neat and decorative on the television but I cannot see it work for me. For one thing, how do you renew the soil after a couple of years? Do you constantly heap compost on to each little bed raising the height each year, or will you need to empty and replace the soil as you do with other containers?

With herbs grown out in the vegetable garden it was always a matter of keeping them under control rather then having to look after them in any other way. Several species of mint and thyme would have taken over large areas if allowed to spread. Fennel and dill seeded themselves with ease – fennel became quite difficult to uproot if left to get too big, but dill was always a pleasure with its decorative yellow flowers. Dill is a herb with two uses – the leaves are specially

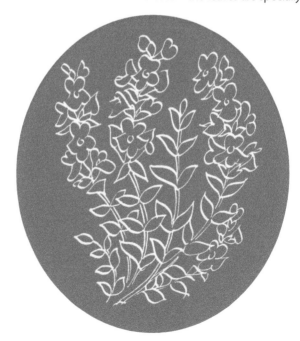

good with fish, with a gentler flavour than that of fennel, and the dried seeds are useful in pickles and for other flavoring, Borage also seeded itself all over the place, and was so decorative that, although we seldom used it I could not bear to uproot it. Other people use the flowers in salads with perhaps nasturtium flowers, and to decorate their glasses of Pimms. You can imagine, from all this, that as I got older the garden looked more and more disorganised, with very few straight lines.

Back to crops; sadly, no more peas or brassicas as explained before, or corn, and also no more carrots. Carrot flies had found my garden and caused a lot of damage. I have tried to grow them in large pots as I am told the pests do not fly higher than eighteen inches. So far I have not succeeded as they either got dried up or drowned in a very rainy summer. That will not stop me from trying again.

Carrots, anyhow are so easily found in shops. They are entirely different from your own young, crunchy, sweet carrots, but have the advantage of keeping well. I would never do this to my own crop, but find that cooking bought carrots with a little butter and a few drops of water in a pyrex dish in the oven works well and preserves the flavour. I also roast them with potatoes and parsnips, or curry any left-overs. Spinach beet still thrives, and needs little attention. Incidentally, I never boil a vegetable that it is possible to steam.

There are probably solutions to many of the various problems that affect my garden after so many years. It would probably mean using various chemicals, but perhaps I am too lazy to find them out. The best solution is not permitted – a rifle to deal with pigeons and squirrels.

Potatoes and onions are still obligingly easy to plant but some other seedlings can be made easier by being played with in the greenhouse. Whereas, years ago, I would have grown leeks in a box, then transplanted the small seedlings straight out, now I do that in the greenhouse. Each leek is popped into a small pot (beetroot too) left to grow strong and tipped into its home later on. I use a conical bulb planting tool that makes it easier for me to handle and the plants seem to grow better too. I still grow a couple of plantings of lettuces up the garden, but of late, keep some back in their boxes in the greenhouse. They may not get such good hearts, but it is sometimes very convenient to have them close by.

I hope to carry on, perhaps with a bit of help. Gardening and growing your own food is not only satisfying, but planning for the next year provides the motivation we all need to get up and go. I cannot imagine a spring without the urge to go out and get my hands in the soil. With your garden, even becoming a little simpler and more limited as you get older, you can still ensure getting most of your own produce to last you throughout the year.

POSTSCRIPT

Just after this book was completed everything changed.
The large garden just became too much. Many of my plants
were getting neglected, they seemed to silently reproach me,
rather like neglected children. My friendly gardener came
once a week, to do the heavier work, but, like all gardeners, he
had his own agenda. It was time to go.

A garden is not your permanent possession. It is for you to
nurture and it in turn nurtures you, and then it must be
handed on. Now the sound of children's voices will again echo
in the garden, and young fingers will help themselves to the
strawberries and pull up the carrots. Their mother wanted
everything left as it was, even all the boxes in the greenhouse.
I will not be there to check up on her, because we have joined
one of our daughters in Australia. Here the windfalls are
oranges and lemons instead of apples, and the love of
gardening which I inherited from my parents has carried on to
the next generation.

Design and production: Mike Blacker, mike@blackerdesign.co.uk
Printed in England